T0090521

# GOD *is the* SOURCE

DANIEL D FREEMAN

WestBow Press books may be ordered through booksellers or by contacting:

WestBow Press
A Division of Thomas Nelson & Zondervan
1663 Liberty Drive
Bloomington, IN 47403
www.westbowpress.com
844-714-3454



ISBN: 979-8-3850-0088-3 (sc)
ISBN: 979-8-3850-0089-0 (e)

Library of Congress Control Number: 2023911195

Print information available on the last page.

WestBow Press rev. date: 06/28/2023

# DEDICATION

This book is dedicated to my mom, Carol Penny Freeman, affectionately known as "Big Penny." Almost from the womb, my mother instilled in me the paramount importance of God's Word. And now that I am old, I have not departed from it and am blessed to be able to share it with others.

# ACKNOWLEDGMENTS

I would first like to thank my beautiful wife and best friend, Janice, without whom the completion of this book would not have happened. Thank you honey for being the best earthly gift God has ever given me. I would also like to thank Emmanuel Baptist Rescue Mission and Gethsemane Baptist Church—two families of faith of which the Lord saw fit to make me a part. Their love and support provided the environment necessary for me to embark upon and complete this journey.

# CONTENTS

# INTRODUCTION

The attributes of God are inexhaustible, but presented to the readers of this book are six attributes of which God alone is the source and makes available to all that place their trust in Him. God desires, and is able, to fulfill our every need. We are created in His image and loved by Him, and there is no good thing He will withhold from us—especially, and primarily speaking, Himself. Through the sacrificial gift of His Son, Jesus Christ, God has made a way for every person who will believe in Him to be made one with Him—the Source of life.

The first and most important need of every human being is the salvation of his or her soul. Through the first human's disobedience to God, we are all inherently born in a spiritually separated state from the Creator of the human race. Thankfully, God provided the solution in the Person of Jesus Christ. He is the only Way to reconciliation with God, and since He was sent to us by God, God is the source of salvation.

God is love, and apart from Him love would not exist in the world. God created people as His center of the universe, and though the first humans disappointed that purpose, God's great love for us conquers that disappointment. Regardless of the severity of pain we may face in this life, we are loved by the Creator of all things, Who has also provided the love of His only begotten Son to be encountered by us through faith in Him.

God's goal for every believing person is to be conformed to the image of His Son. True joy comes as a result of surrendering to God's goal. For the joy of reconciling doomed sinners to God, Jesus Christ endured and surrendered Himself on the cross. Though not easy by any means, it is the believer's reasonable service to surrender to God's plans for his or her life, and thereby walk in the inexplicable joy only God supplies.

Jesus Christ, Who is alive and seated at the right hand of the Father, has provided total access to God's Throne for every believer. Prayer is the vehicle through which this access is utilized. There is divine peace of which only God is the source—peace which surpasses our human understanding. Through sincere prayer, in Jesus Christ's name, God's peace is made available to every believer for daily living. Like Daniel in the lions' den, any believer walking in the peace of God is able to face the fiercest obstacles.

God cannot lie, which makes Him the only source of certain hope. As we look at the world around us, seeming hopelessness abounds. But the believer is instructed to look up because the believer's hope is not of this world.

God Himself is hope that never fails, dies nor disappoints. The reality of eternal life in Jesus Christ is the anchor of hope in which every believer is to be grounded.

God is good and can never be approached as being separate from His goodness. Because we live in a fallen world, even as believers, we will experience things that aren't good. But God is. The first deception in the earth came by way of doubting God's goodness. But the truth, for every believer, is the comfort of God's goodness is always available in every situation or circumstance. Whether created by our own decisions or uncontrollable external sources, trouble can be endured by the believer because the very nature of the One to Whom we belong is good.

I pray the following six easy-to-read chapters will encourage and strengthen you by reminding you that the One to Whom you belong is your Source of Salvation, Love, Joy, Peace, Hope and Goodness if you have accepted His eternally living gift in the Person of Jesus Christ. To the reader which perhaps has not yet accepted Jesus Christ as personal Lord and Savior, I pray reading this book will help you see—and more importantly, hear—the one and only Truth, Who is also the one and only Source.

Chapter
# ONE

# GOD IS THE SOURCE OF SALVATION

*"For all have sinned, and come short of the glory of God;" Romans 3:23 KJV*

All humans—from Adam to you and me—have sinned and come (or fall) short of God's glory. Through the first man's disobedience to his Creator's instruction, we all enter this world in an inherent state of dissatisfaction with God's righteousness, holiness, and purity.

It is God's desire, however, to be satisfied with us, and give us hearts that are satisfied with Him rather than with the sinful pleasures of this world. Only God can make this change of heart, known as salvation, take place in a person. Therefore, God is the source of salvation for every human being.

Before Earth was created and time began, a decision was made in eternity to provide salvation for all mankind. This salvation is a Person, and His name is Jesus Christ. The bible says:

> *"In the beginning was the Word, and the Word was with God, and the Word was God. The same was in the beginning with God. All things were made by him; and without him was not any thing made that was made. In him was life; and the life was the light of men. John 1:1-4 KJV*

> *"And the Word was made flesh, and dwelt among us, (and we beheld his glory, the glory as of the only begotten of the Father,) full of grace and truth." John 1:14 KJV*

The Word which "was made flesh" is Jesus Christ. Verse four of the above passage says, "In him was life; and the life was the light of men." Through the first human's disobedience to God, all of mankind is born in spiritual darkness. Jesus Christ is the life which lights men (and women, and children). Man does not light himself and is totally incapable of doing so. Regardless of behavior, every person's natural state is one of spiritual blindness, and the solution is not found within us, but in God.

Staying in the gospel according to John, we find in chapter four an account given of a very personal, and intentional, encounter between Jesus and a woman of Samaria at Jacob's well. The bible says, beginning at John 4:7:

> *"There cometh a woman of Samaria to draw water: Jesus saith unto her, 'Give me to drink.' (For his disciples were gone away unto the city to buy meat.) Then saith the woman of Samaria unto him, 'How is it that thou, being a Jew, askest drink of me, which am a woman of Samaria?' for the Jews have no dealings with the Samaritans. Jesus answered and said unto her, 'If thou knewest the gift of God, and who it is that saith to thee, Give me to drink; thou wouldest have asked of him, and he would have given thee living water.'" John 4:7-10 KJV*

Jesus described His living water (His life-giving power) as "the gift of God." Salvation is a gift. It is impossible for mankind to earn or muster up self-qualifying morality for the salvation only God has the power to give. God only requires a person to realize his or her need for salvation, and sincerely ask Him for it. The bible refers to this as grace, and says, beginning at Ephesians 2:4:

> *"But God, who is rich in mercy, for his great love wherewith he loved us, even when we were dead in sins, hath quickened us together with Christ, (by grace ye are saved;) and hath raised us up together, and made us sit together in heavenly places in Christ Jesus: that in the ages to come he might shew the exceeding riches of his grace in his kindness toward us through Christ Jesus. For by grace are ye saved through faith; and that not of yourselves: it is the gift of God:" Ephesians 2:4-8 KJV*

God's rich mercy and great love are the motivators through which His grace is provided, not any righteousness from within us. The word translated as "quickened" in verse five means "made us alive." You have most likely, at some point during your life, heard the phrase, "Dead man walking." An individual who has not accepted God's gift of salvation in the Person of Jesus Christ is, quite literally, a dead man (or woman) walking. The bible says:

> *"For the wages of sin is death; but the gift of God is eternal life through Jesus Christ our Lord." Romans 6:23 KJV*

Notice in the above verse that death is earned (wages), but eternal life is given (gift). Jesus Christ Himself said:

> *"Come unto me, all ye that labour and are heavy laden, and I will give you rest." Matthew 11:28 KJV*

He also famously told Nicodemus:

> *"For God so loved the world, that he gave his only begotten Son, that whosoever believeth in him should not perish, but have everlasting life." John 3:16 KJV*

Salvation being given, not earned, is the emphasis of the above Scriptures. These verses, as well as a host of others, make clear the truth that the only way of escape from the spiritual death and darkness humans are born in is God Himself. Charitable deeds, acts of kindness, living a generally moral life and raising our children to do the same, are not avenues to heaven or salvation. God alone, through the willing sacrifice and shed blood of Jesus, is the source of salvation for every person born into this planet.

June 22, 1997 is a most important date in my life. It is the day the Lord saved my soul. When I woke up that morning, the very last thing on my mind was giving my life to Christ. I had been partying the night before and was planning to continue once I cleared the formality of attending Sunday service. I was born and raised in the church and had attended the same church my entire life up to that point. But the lure of social acceptance pulled me into the bar scene. Unbeknownst to me, God was ready to give me a gift that day—the gift of a heart softened to receive His grace. For the first time in my life, a worship song by the choir brought tears to my eyes, and as the saying goes, the rest is history. When the sermon was ended, and the offer to accept Christ was made, I found my legs walking my body to the altar. Through that day's singing and sermon, God's grace penetrated my heart, and the kindness of Him to soften my heart was irresistible.

God is not only the source of salvation, but also the source of what sustains a person subsequent to his or her conversion. Peter, one of Jesus Christ's most prominent apostles, wrote in his first epistle:

> *"Blessed be the God and Father of our Lord Jesus Christ, which according to his abundant mercy hath begotten us again unto a lively hope by the resurrection of Jesus Christ from the dead, to an*

> *inheritance incorruptible, and undefiled, and that fadeth not away, reserved in heaven for you, who are kept by the power of God through faith unto salvation ready to be revealed in the last time." 1 Peter 1:3-5 KJV*

The believer is "kept by the power of God." Once saved, God uniquely calls His children to serve Him in severally different ways and capacities. However, the good works executed by believers for the advancement of God's kingdom are not what keep them—God's power does. The bible says:

> *"For it is God which worketh in you both to will and to do of his good pleasure." Philippians 2:13 KJV*

The desire to do and the doing of good works are both wrought in the believer by God. This is great news because God does not want us pressuring ourselves to "impress" Him. That's not possible. We are to rest in what Jesus Christ has accomplished for us and serve Him with gladness and peace.

Perhaps you are reading this and have never accepted the gift of salvation in the Person of Jesus Christ. My heart was softened in one day, but maybe you've been feeling a wooing for some time now. The bible says:

> *"That if thou shalt confess with thy mouth the Lord Jesus, and shalt believe in thine heart that God hath raised him from the dead, thou shalt be saved. For with the heart man believeth unto righteousness; and with the mouth confession is made unto salvation. For the scripture saith, 'Whosoever believeth on him shall not be ashamed.'" Romans 10:9-11 KJV*

If the words of the above passage are pulling on your heart, I implore you to take action. God loves you.

To the believer, we all should be reminded from time to time that God is the One Who has put us into right relationship with Him. It is possible to become what I refer to as being "churched," and unintentionally wander from our first love through a multitude of busyness. But God is faithful and unceasing in His desire for intimate oneness. He is the One that saves us. He is the One that keeps us. He is the One that performs His good pleasure through us. He is the Source.

# Chapter TWO

# GOD IS THE SOURCE OF LOVE

*"In this was manifested the love of God toward us, because that God sent his only begotten Son into the world, that we might live through him. Herein is love, not that we loved God, but that he loved us, and sent his Son to be the propitiation for our sins."*
*1 John 4:9-10 KJV*

What does the bible mean when it says Jesus Christ is the "only begotten Son" of God? It means Jesus is the only holy human being to ever be birthed into this world. God is holy (1 Peter 1:15-16), and holiness begets holiness. Jesus was sent to us by God to willingly sacrifice his holy and blameless life on a cruel and shameful cross—the totally innocent and undeserving dying an exceedingly excruciating death for the totally guilty and deserving. "Herein is love."

In today's society, love is a word used for a myriad of things. "I love my favorite football team. I love these new pair of shoes." In reality, love exists in the world at all because God is love, and He created the world. The bible says:

> *"Beloved, let us love one another: for love is of God; and every one that loveth is born of God, and knoweth God. He that loveth not knoweth not God; for God is love." 1 John 4:7-8 KJV*

These two verses precede the two verses quoted to open this chapter. When taken all together, we see that God is not only the origin and source of love, but that He also displayed His love in the highest form possible. Jesus said to His disciples:

> *"Greater love hath no man than this, that a man lay down his life for his friends." John 15:13 KJV*

Interesting that Jesus would define man's optimum display of love this way, considering:

> *"But God commendeth his love toward us, in that, while we were yet sinners, Christ died for us." Romans 5:8 KJV*

A sinner is not God's friend, yet He gave all sinners His only begotten Son. This goes far beyond the definition Jesus provided for His disciples. This is important to understand because, many times, we may downgrade God's love for us through the lens of pain caused to us by other people. The hurts we experience as a result of living in a fallen world are not to serve as any sort of standard by which to measure or view God's love.

The bible says the love of Christ passes knowledge (Ephesians 3:19), but that it is possible to know the love of Christ. How can something that passes knowledge still be known? God's love is not something to be comprehended with human intellect, but rather through encounter. Jesus said about Himself:

> *"The Spirit of the Lord is upon me, because he hath anointed me to preach the gospel*

> *to the poor; he hath sent me to heal the brokenhearted, to preach deliverance to the captives, and recovering of sight to the blind, to set at liberty them that are bruised," Luke 4:18 KJV*

Most rational people love their parents, their spouse, and their children dearly, but no one except God can love as described in the above verse. God is a Spirit (John 4:24), and He being love, loves us spiritually—from the inside out, with the power to heal all wounds and heartache. When we become believers in Jesus Christ, God places His Spirit inside of us, providing us the capacity to love as He loves—a love capable even of loving one's enemies. This is unconditional, supernatural love that has God alone as its source.

My parents separated while my mom was pregnant with me. Though my dad was somewhat in my life, and took me to see many professional sporting events, it wasn't nearly the experience a child has of living in the home with a loving father. As I entered my teenage years and young adulthood, I became a heavy drinker. At the time, I thought I was more attracted to partying than most people. But looking back, it was definitely connected to the void left by a fatherless home, which I was attempting to fill with my own vices.

There are many ways in which people may be wounded during childhood and carry those wounds into adulthood. On the surface things may appear normal, but deep within the heart and soul—where only God can see and gain access—a person's wounds may still be left unhealed and even gaping. Jesus said He was sent to heal the brokenhearted, and guess what? Jesus knows each and every person before he or she is ever conceived in the womb (Jeremiah 1:5). God loves us with a foreknowledge of our lives from beginning to end. God knew my parents would separate during my mom's pregnancy, and He knows whatever may be ailing you.

For most of my life, I accused my dad of abandoning his responsibilities because he didn't want me in the first place. But before my dad passed away, God saved him and reconciled us. Nothing is too hard for God. His love resurrected Jesus Christ from the dead.

This may be hard for some to accept, but apart from Christ, it is impossible to love from a position of purity. Jesus said:

> *"I am the true vine, and my Father is the husbandman. Every branch in me that beareth not fruit he taketh away: and every branch that beareth fruit, he purgeth it, that it may bring forth more fruit. Now ye are clean through the word which I have spoken unto you. Abide in me, and I in you. As the branch cannot bear fruit of itself, except it abide in the vine; no more can ye,*

> *except ye abide in me. I am the vine, ye are the branches: He that abideth in me, and I in him, the same bringeth forth much fruit: for without me ye can do nothing." John 15:1-5 KJV*

For many years I associated this passage with good works. But in reality, Jesus is speaking in the context of love. He continues:

> *"Herein is my Father glorified, that ye bear much fruit; so shall ye be my disciples. As the Father hath loved me, so have I loved you: continue ye in my love. If ye keep my commandments, ye shall abide in my love; even as I have kept my Father's commandments, and abide in his love. These things have I spoken unto you, that my joy might remain in you, and that your joy might be full. This is my commandment, That ye love one another, as I have loved you. John 15:8-12 KJV*

> *"Ye have not chosen me, but I have chosen you, and ordained you, that ye should go and bring forth fruit, and that your fruit should remain: that whatsoever ye shall ask of the Father in my name, he may give it*

*you. These things I command you, that ye love one another." John 15:16-17 KJV*

The foremost "fruit" the believer is to bring forth is love. Jesus said we can do nothing (of true and eternal value) without Him. So apart from Him, this foremost fruit of love cannot be produced. Jesus also stated we have not chosen Him, but He has chosen us. We did not seek the Source; the Source sought us. We are sought and bought by love through the blood of Jesus Christ.

God created us as beings of relationship, and in the heart of God, the only true way to relate is in love. Love is an act of the will and is oftentimes inconvenient. Jesus Christ inconvenienced Himself beyond what human intelligence is capable of grasping. He is the Source of love, and compassionately invites us all to be supplied of Him.

# Chapter THREE

# GOD IS THE SOURCE OF JOY

*"Looking unto Jesus the author and finisher of our faith; who for the joy that was set before him endured the cross, despising the shame, and is set down at the right hand of the throne of God." Hebrews 12:2 KJV*

Have you ever heard that happiness is based on circumstances, but joy is not? Jesus Christ faced the greatest circumstance in human history and endured it, "for the joy that was set before him." The joy of reconciling doomed sinners to God was the source from which Jesus drew strength to endure the cross. His joy was found in an intended end—a goal.

Most people set meaningful goals for themselves, but God also has a goal:

> *"For whom he did foreknow, he also did predestinate to be conformed to the image of his Son, that he might be the firstborn among many brethren." Romans 8:29 KJV*

God's goal for every believing person is "to be conformed to the image of his Son." Jesus surrendered Himself on the cross for the joy that awaited Him on the other side. Likewise, the more we surrender to God's goal of conforming us to the image of His Son, the more of His joy we will ultimately experience. Joy comes from and is found in God, but contrary to popular belief, joy is based on a circumstance—surrender.

As is the case with most things stemming from God's infinite wisdom, joy through surrender contradicts the natural mind. This is why the bible says:

> *"Fulfil ye my joy, that ye be likeminded, having the same love, being of one accord, of one mind. Philippians 2:2 KJV*

> *"Let this mind be in you, which was also in Christ Jesus: who, being in the form of God, thought it not robbery to be equal with God: but made himself of no reputation, and took upon him the form of a servant, and was made in the likeness of men: and being found in fashion as a man, he humbled himself, and became obedient unto death, even the death of the cross. Wherefore God also hath highly exalted him, and given him a name which is above every name: that at the name of Jesus every knee should bow, of things in heaven, and things in earth, and things under the earth; and that every tongue should confess that Jesus Christ is Lord, to the glory of God the Father." Philippians 2:5-11 KJV*

One of the most fascinating Old Testament stories is the story of Joseph. Here we find a teenage boy chosen by God for multinational greatness. God communicated His plans for Joseph's future greatness to him through dreams. Like any of us would most likely be, Joseph was excited to receive revelation from God concerning his future, and in his young naivety, shared the dreams with his already jealous brothers. Even his father Jacob—who was not guiltless in overtly favoring Joseph above his other sons—was not quite ready for the God-given vision (Genesis 37:3-11).

The story goes on to tell how Joseph's brothers' animosity toward him escalated to such a level where they successfully conspired to sell Joseph into slavery in the land of Egypt. Once a slave, Joseph still walked in God's favor. The bible even says that as a slave, Joseph "was a prosperous man" (Genesis 39:2 KJV). Over time, his master's wife became infatuated with Joseph and pursued him daily for a sexual affair. But Joseph refused, until ultimately, his master's wife tried to physically force him, and he fled leaving his garment behind (Genesis 39:7-12). With garment in hand, the immoral wife concocted a lie accusing Joseph of sexual assault. The accusation landed Joseph in prison, where once again, the Lord was with him (Genesis 39:21). He became the assistant to the keeper of the prison. As a result, he was eventually assigned the responsibility of looking after two of the Egyptian king's servants, who had been charged with offenses of their own (Genesis 40:1-4).

As it turns out, the Egyptian king's servants both had dreams one night, which Joseph, through God's gifting, was able to interpret for them—each man his dream. Joseph's interpretations were that one would be set free and restored, the other sentenced to execution. Both interpretations came to pass, but the butler—the freed servant—forgot Joseph when he was restored to his post (Genesis 40:5-23).

After two full years, the bible says, the Egyptian king, Pharaoh, dreamed two dreams which greatly troubled him. Not one of his servants was able to interpret them for him. Then the butler remembered Joseph, and shared with Pharaoh his experience with Joseph in the prison and how his dream was correctly interpreted by him. Pharaoh immediately called for Joseph, and he—through God's gifting—interpreted the dreams for Pharaoh. Both dreams contained the same meaning: seven years of plenty followed by seven years of famine for the land of Egypt and surrounding lands. Not only that, but God had given Joseph wisdom in determining the solution for the impending disaster. As a result, Joseph, a Hebrew slave and inmate, was made second in command only behind Pharaoh and successfully navigated the land of Egypt through the disaster.

God used Joseph to save many lives, including the lives of his father and brothers who had sold him years earlier. Joseph was also given a wife by Pharaoh with whom he fathered two children. The names Joseph gave his two sons are really the reason his story was briefly recounted here. The bible tells us:

> *"And unto Joseph were born two sons before the years of famine came, which Asenath the daughter of Poti-pherah priest of On bare unto him. And Joseph called the name of the firstborn Manasseh: 'For God,' said*

> *he, 'hath made me forget all my toil, and all my father's house.' And the name of the second called he Ephraim: 'For God hath caused me to be fruitful in the land of my affliction.'" Genesis 41:50-52 KJV*

Somehow, through all of his injustices, Joseph was able to remain in a surrendered posture to God's ultimate plans for his life. Joseph's faith in God, and what God revealed to him as a teenage boy, was so firm that it anchored him to endure the harshest of trials. The eventual joy Joseph experienced was so exceedingly great, that it influenced the naming of his children. We can see in Joseph's story how God used the wickedness of his brothers for Joseph's ultimate good. God turned his affliction into joy.

Most times while going through trials, it isn't so joyful. But the bible says even before we experience tangible joy, we can by faith "count it all joy" (James 1:2 KJV). Most scholars agree that Joseph was a "type" of Christ—a foreshadowing of Christ's character. If this is indeed the case, we see that surrendering to God's plans, through trust in His faithfulness, leads to ultimate joy.

As believers, there is joy in having our sins washed away, but there is also joy to be received during and after extremely challenging seasons in our lives. Like Joseph, this is where surrender comes in—believing that God is working all things into His ultimate plans for our lives. Though living a multitude of centuries prior to the arrival of Jesus, Joseph exhibited the mind of Christ. And we are called to do the same. This is not easy by any means and requires diligent, sincere prayer and a commitment to trust God's promises. What Jesus endured on the cross is unfathomable, but it happened. And it happened because He loves us, and for the joy which awaited Him across the finish line:

> *"Weeping may endure for a night, but joy cometh in the morning." Psalm 30:5b KJV*

# Chapter FOUR

# GOD IS THE SOURCE OF PEACE

*"Be careful for nothing; but in every thing by prayer and supplication with thanksgiving let your requests be made known unto God. And the peace of God, which passeth all understanding, shall keep your hearts and minds through Christ Jesus." Philippians 4:6-7 KJV*

Jesus said the peace He gives is not as the world gives (John 14:27). So apparently, there is an earthly peace which may be attained. That peace, however, is immeasurably inferior to the peace of God, because the peace of God is promised to surpass our human understanding. This is similar to the love of Christ surpassing human knowledge.

In the previous chapter, we looked at surrender as being a required condition to experiencing God's joy. Similarly, the bible provides us certain prerequisites necessary to enjoy God's peace:

"Be careful for nothing; but in every thing by prayer and supplication (give all anxieties to God through prayer) with thanksgiving (and with a heart of gratitude) let your requests be made known unto God (be truthful and transparent, trusting in God's compassion)."

We are promised that if we approach God's Throne of grace and mercy in this way, He will keep (or guard) our hearts and minds with His peace "through Christ Jesus" (the Holy Spirit within us). When we trust Jesus as Lord and Savior of our souls, He makes our spiritual standing one of peace with God the Father (Romans 5:1). But it is also necessary to have the peace which God provides in the daily living of this life's situations and circumstances.

Most people, if even in a general sense, are familiar with the story of Daniel in the lions' den. Daniel was a praying man—a quality his enemies used against him in an attempt to have him destroyed. The bible tells us that when Daniel knew a thirty-day royal statute had been decreed prohibiting all inhabitants of the land to pray to anyone but the king, Daniel "*knelt down on his knees three times that day, and prayed and gave thanks before his God, as was his custom since early days." (Daniel 6:10 NKJV)*

The punishment for anyone that violated the thirty-day royal statute was a dinner date with the den of lions. But Daniel refused to bow or pray to anyone but the one true God. When Daniel's haters found him praying, they reported it to the king, who was regretfully obligated to follow through with the statute. The bible says:

> *"Then the king commanded, and they brought Daniel, and cast him into the den of lions. Now the king spake and said unto Daniel, 'Thy God whom thou servest continually, he will deliver thee.'" Daniel 6:16 KJV*

I think it's important to note here before we go on in the story, that Daniel's devotion to God was greatly observed by those around him. Daniel's enemies knew the decree would not stop him from praying to God. They observed Daniel's walk with God—it was so strong, even the threat of being thrown into the den of lions would not alter his devotion. Then we have the king, whom once he realized it was Daniel who had violated the decree, was remorseful, and did everything he could to try to stop it (Daniel 6:14). The king's observance of Daniel's walk with God led him to believe God would deliver Daniel from the lions!

When we live in God's peace, it is very noticeable to those around us—especially unbelievers who may know we are believers. Like it or not, believers are observed by those within their immediate circles because we are "a peculiar people" (Titus 2:14 KJV). Listen to the effect the peace of God within Daniel had on the king:

> *"Then the king went to his palace, and passed the night fasting: neither were instruments of musick brought before him: and his sleep went from him. Then the king arose very early in the morning, and went in haste unto the den of lions. And when he came to the den, he cried with a lamentable voice unto Daniel, 'O Daniel, servant of the living God, is thy God, whom thou servest continually able to deliver thee from the lions?' Then said Daniel unto the king, 'O king, live for ever. My God hath sent his angel, and hath shut the lions' mouths, that they have not hurt me: forasmuch as before him innocency was found in me; and also before thee, O king, have I done no hurt.' Then was the king exceeding glad for him, and commanded that they should take Daniel*

> *up out of the den. So Daniel was taken up out of the den, and no manner of hurt was found upon him, because he believed in his God. And the king commanded, and they brought those men which had accused Daniel, and they cast them into the den of lions, them, their children, and their wives; and the lions had the mastery of them, and brake all their bones in pieces or ever they came at the bottom of the den." Daniel 6:18-24 KJV*

Peace that keeps a person from fearing a den of lions is peace which passes all understanding. The believer's enemy, the devil, has all sorts of dens and lions with which he attempts to paralyze the believer with fear. He is after all himself described as "a roaring lion" walking about "seeking whom he may devour" (1 Peter 5:8 KJV).

If you read Daniel's story in its entirety, you will see that God greatly promoted Daniel multiple times. But Daniel's peace was not found in promotions or status. It was found in God. When the time of testing came—where Daniel faced losing everything including his life—he did not waver, but ran to the only true safety anyone really has.

Riches, status, a happy marriage and well behaved children are not evil things to have. They are good. But to look to those things for your peace in life is not wise.

If ever a time arrives when, like Daniel, none of those things can rescue you or provide peace, you have a God in heaven that has already promised you peace, both here and eternally, in the safety of His Son.

Jesus Christ has given every believer total access to approach God's Throne in prayer. We are to boldly use this vehicle as a means of running to our Father in all circumstances—good and bad—to receive His peace. The world, and the situations we sometimes face as inhabitants of it, cannot take the peace of God away from the believer. Like Daniel, we are uniquely equipped to face the fiercest of challenges. We have peace with and in God through Jesus Christ Who paid our debt on the cross. Let us rest in Him, for He is the Source of true and eternal peace.

You may be saying, "Brother Freeman, you don't know the kinds of things I'm facing right now. It's easy to write, 'Have peace.'" You're right; I don't know the kinds of things you may be facing right now. But I know God, and the promises of God are eternally true. The emotions we experience, including fear and anxiety, are all too real and very convincing at times. But God knows our frame and remembers that we are dust (Psalm 103:14). There is power in crying out to God. It's not always easy, but He's real, He's there, and He wants to supply us His peace in the midst.

I grew up watching my mother raise, work and provide for four children. Sometimes we lived in relative comfort, and sometimes we lived in lesser comfort. But two things always stayed the same—going to church, and my mom never calling in sick. She was, and still is, a praying woman, and I never once saw life's circumstances overtake her. She was overtaken by her relationship with Jesus. Her conversations always led to Jesus, and He was, and still is, her Source. She was very comfortable and unafraid when it came to witnessing to unbelievers, and no matter what, she was always thankful. She told me she named me Daniel because of what she went through while pregnant with me. And looking back, I definitely see how Daniel's story impacted her approach to life. The peace of God is real and available, and only a prayer away:

> *"And let the peace of God rule in your hearts, to the which also ye are called in one body; and be ye thankful." Colossians 3:15 KJV*

Chapter

# FIVE

# GOD IS THE SOURCE OF HOPE

*"May God, the source of hope, fill you with joy and peace through your faith in him. Then you will overflow with hope by the power of the Holy Spirit." Romans 15:13 GW*

I hope the Pittsburgh Steelers—my favorite professional sports franchise—win a seventh Super Bowl title during my lifetime. But that kind of hope is not the hope God is and provides. The Apostle Paul, in his encouraging epistle of instruction to young pastor Titus, opens the letter with these words:

> *"Paul, a servant of God, and an apostle of Jesus Christ, according to the faith of God's elect, and the acknowledging of the truth which is after godliness; in hope of eternal life, which God, that cannot lie, promised before the world began;" Titus 1:1-2 KJV*

There is a lot being said within the first two verses of Paul's epistle to Titus, but let us focus on Paul's context of hope in verse two. In this context, hope is confidence that a promise from God, Who cannot lie, will come to pass. This hope is certain and sure to happen. It is guaranteed because God cannot lie. God is the only Person that cannot lie. Many people live honest lives, but it's still possible for them to lie. It's possible for any of us to lie. But with God, it is impossible to lie. There is a difference between not doing something and not being able to do something. God is holy, and the bible says He cannot lie, assuring us that it is absolutely impossible for the One that created you and me to ever speak anything other than the truth.

But there's more to the definition of hope as used in the above context. To paraphrase, Paul was saying that his life as a servant of God and apostle of Jesus Christ was lived in hope. This means living daily in the confidence that what God has promised, He will do. It also means living in the confidence of your calling. The ultimate promise of God to every believer is eternal life, so the hope written of in the above passage is available to—and should be lived in by—all believers.

The bible tells us God Himself is hope to all those that place their trust in Him. Jeremiah put it this way:

> *"Blessed is the man that trusteth in the LORD, and whose hope the LORD is." Jeremiah 17:7 KJV*

God is the only true source of hope. The world and its system has a counterfeit offering for almost every attribute of God, but the bible is clear in reminding believers of the severe situation we were saved from:

> *"That at that time ye were without Christ, being aliens from the commonwealth of Israel, and strangers from the covenants of promise, having no hope, and without God in the world: But now in Christ Jesus ye who sometimes were far off are made nigh by the blood of Christ." Ephesians 2:12-13 KJV*

A person may own the largest house on the block and possess a net worth of millions, but without God that person is hopeless. Before accepting Jesus Christ as personal Savior, each and every one of us was hopeless, but praise God for His mercy, grace and incomprehensible love!

It is pretty much impossible for Satan to make a believer hopeless, but that doesn't stop the devil from trying. He had a single goal in mind concerning Job—to cause Job to curse God (Job 1:11). The enemy of your soul and mine will bring people and situations against us in an attempt to deceive us into thinking God doesn't care, but God is faithful and in control. The psalmist wrote:

> *"As with a sword in my bones, mine enemies reproach me; while they say daily unto me, 'Where is thy God?' Why art thou cast down, O my soul? and why art thou disquieted within me? hope thou in God: for I shall yet praise him, who is the health of my countenance, and my God." Psalm 42:10-11 KJV*

Times of disappointment, emotional downturn, and even pain, will come. But the hope God is and provides gives us confidence through which we "shall yet praise him." Praise is a weapon enlivened by the hope of God against spiritual opposition.

Let us take a look at the opening verse to this chapter, but in the King James Version:

> *"Now the God of hope fill you with all joy and peace in believing, that ye may abound in hope, through the power of the Holy Ghost." Romans 15:13 KJV*

A person that believes in God—and more specifically that He sent Jesus Christ to save us from our sins—is at any given moment in the best possible condition he or she can be in. In the above verse we are told that God desires to fill us with joy and peace because we believe in Him. Situations and life circumstances will attempt to dictate your joy and peace. But God says the simple fact that you trust and believe in Him will cause Him to "fill you with all joy and peace in believing." We see here the basis for the believer's joy and peace is not situations and life circumstances, but belief in God. The verse continues, that being filled with God's joy and peace in believing, "ye may abound in hope, through the power of the Holy Ghost."

We saw earlier that hope is synonymous with confidence. God wants us to abound in hope—abound in confidence that God is Who He says He is. The Holy Spirit within the believer bears witness to Who God is and is also the Person of the Godhead that teaches the believer who he or she truly is in Christ (Romans 8:16). The bible says:

> *"Beloved, now are we the sons of God, and it doth not yet appear what we shall be: but we know that, when he shall appear, we shall be like him; for we shall see him as he is. And every man that hath this hope in him purifieth himself, even as he is pure."*
> *1 John 3:2-3 KJV*

If you are a believer, it is imperative for you to know on a daily basis, you are God's child. Your name is written in Heaven, and you will live with Jesus, bodily, forever. It is currently not manifest what we as believers ultimately are, "but we know that, when he shall appear, we shall be like him; for we shall see him as he is." There is a day in which every believer will be made as perfect in body and soul as is already the case in spirit—glorified. This is not a myth. It is a promise from God. It is a real and eternal destination for every believer.

Hopeless is the very last thing any believer in Jesus Christ is. God is calling you to live each day in the confidence of the truth that you belong to Him, and your eternal state is secure. It is fairly easy to be distracted by what needs to be done in this life in order to live in some semblance of security. But the believer's Source of hope is the One that is beyond, and not of, this world.

Mass shootings, inexplicable viruses, human trafficking and constant reports of pending wars are just a few of the daily news stories that speak hopelessness to the world. But if you're a believer, the truth is you belong to and serve God. Believers do not belong to nor do they serve this world or the darkness which captivates it. As believers, we need to remind one another that this world is not our home. Yes, I greatly desire to see my Steelers win another Lombardi Trophy, even with all the pain going on in the world. But ten more Lombardi Trophies can absolutely not bring me the hope I already have in Christ Jesus.

Do you currently have loved ones trapped in addictions? Hope in the living God. Are your career and personal finances not where they used to be? Hope in the living God. Is your marriage deteriorating or your children rebelling? Hope in the living God. God has not stopped caring, and He will never stop caring. On the cross, and in His humanity, Jesus asked God the Father the reason for His seeming abandonment (Matthew 27:46). But Jesus was not abandoned and neither are you. And if it's been a while since someone prayed for you, let me just remind you that my prayer for you is one of confidence:

> *"For the hope which is laid up for you in heaven, whereof ye heard before in the word of the truth of the gospel;" Colossians 1:5 KJV*

# Chapter SIX

# GOD IS THE SOURCE OF GOODNESS

*"Beloved, follow not that which is evil, but that which is good. He that doeth good is of God: but he that doeth evil hath not seen God." 3 John 11 KJV*

In Genesis chapter three we learn about the fall of man. This tragic incident with eternal consequences began with a seed of doubt being planted concerning God's goodness. The bible says:

> *"Now the serpent was more subtil than any beast of the field which the LORD God had made. And he said unto the woman, 'Yea, hath God said, Ye shall not eat of every tree of the garden?' And the woman said unto the serpent, 'We may eat of the fruit of the trees of the garden: but of the fruit of the tree which is in the midst of the garden, God hath said, Ye shall not eat of it, neither shall ye touch it, lest ye die.' And the serpent said unto the woman, 'Ye shall not surely die: for God doth know that in the day ye eat thereof, then your eyes shall be opened, and ye shall be as gods, knowing good and evil.' And when the woman saw that the tree was good for food, and that it was pleasant to the eyes, and a tree to be desired to make one wise, she took of the fruit thereof, and did eat, and gave also unto her husband with her; and he did eat." Genesis 3:1-6 KJV*

The tactic used by the serpent, the devil, was falsely accusing God of withholding something good from Eve and her husband. But the truth is:

> *"For the LORD God is a sun and shield: the LORD will give grace and glory: no good thing will he withhold from them that walk uprightly. O LORD of hosts, blessed is the man that trusteth in thee." Psalm 84:11-12 KJV*

The devil, Satan, attacked Eve's trust in God and attacks every believer's trust in God to this day. But God is good and trustworthy at all times. As mentioned in the previous chapter, God cannot lie, so when He tells us to do something, or not do something, we can always trust Him. God is the exact opposite of what Satan accused Him of in the garden, for the bible says:

> *"And we know that all things work together for good to them that love God, to them who are the called according to his purpose. For whom he did foreknow, he also did predestinate to be conformed to the image of his Son, that he might be the firstborn among many brethren. Moreover whom he did predestinate, them he also called: and whom he called, them he also justified: and whom he justified, them he also glorified. What shall we then say to these things? If God be for us, who can be against us? He that spared not his own Son, but delivered*

> *him up for us all, how shall he not with him also freely give us all things?" Romans 8:28-32 KJV*

In chapter one I mentioned the decision to provide salvation for all mankind was made before Earth was created. God knew, before creating Earth and man, the fall would happen. The bible states that Jesus Christ is "the Lamb slain from the foundation of the world" (Revelation 13:8 KJV). Only a good God would provide a way of rescue for a people He foreknew would fall through disobedience.

In the gospels according to Matthew, Mark and Luke, we are told of an encounter between Jesus and a man often termed as the rich young ruler. The bible says:

> *"And when he was gone forth into the way, there came one running, and kneeled to him, and asked him, 'Good Master, what shall I do that I may inherit eternal life?' And Jesus said unto him, 'Why callest thou me good? there is none good but one, that is, God.'" Mark 10:17-18 KJV*

Jesus, in His humanity, declared to the man that the only good One is God. As believers, we know Jesus Christ and the Father are One (John 10:30), but Jesus humbled Himself and lived on the earth as a full man serving God.

Jesus lived His entire life without sin, so if He said God is good, God is good.

There is another lesson to be learned from the exchange between Jesus and the "rich young ruler." Jesus asked the man why it was he called Him good—the reason being only God is good. Here was an opportunity for the man to confess the reason he called Jesus good was because Jesus is God. But apparently he did not recognize Who it was standing before him. If he had, he probably would have been obedient to sell all he had, give to the poor and follow Jesus. But in the recorded accounts of Matthew, Mark and Luke, he missed his opportunity. Perhaps at a later unrecorded time, the man did follow Jesus. We can only ponder. What are you calling Jesus, and Who is Jesus to you? Is He good? Is He God? Is He your Source?

God cannot be separated from His goodness. The events we experience in this life are not indicators of whether God is good or not good in various situations. God is always good, because goodness is Who God is. The goodness of God is what leads sinners to repentance (Romans 2:4), and apart from God pure goodness is nonexistent.

When God's Word commands us to fear Him, He is not commanding us to fear Him in the sense of being afraid to approach Him. On the contrary, the more we approach God through prayer, meditation, and study of His Word, the more of His goodness we experience.

Ultimately, God has good plans for our overall lives. Sometimes we fall short, and God, being the loving Father He is, corrects us. But ultimately, He only wants what is best for our lives, and that best comes from Him.

We read in the Old Testament, many times over, how the people of Israel and Judah were subdued and taken captive by other nations because of disobedience. But even then, God in His goodness watched over them. It may be considered the seventy-year exile to Babylon was the most pivotal of these seasons of correction. But listen to the message God sent to them while in captivity through the pen of Jeremiah the prophet:

> *"This is what the LORD says: 'You will be in Babylon for seventy years. But then I will come and do for you all the good things I have promised, and I will bring you home again. For I know the plans I have for you,' says the LORD. 'They are plans for good and not for disaster, to give you a future and a hope. In those days when you pray, I will listen. If you look for me wholeheartedly, you will find me. I will be found by you,' says the LORD. 'I will end your captivity and restore your fortunes. I will gather you out of the nations where I sent you and will bring you home again to your own land.'"*
> *Jeremiah 29:10-14 NLT*

God is good even when our own disobedience brings trouble and harm into our lives. God is just, so there are times when unwise and sinful decisions will result in very dire consequences. If you're reading this and are in the midst of troubled circumstances, whether due to your own decisions or uncontrollable external sources, the fact that you're still breathing means God's goodness is still at work in your life. Confess all to God with a sincere heart of repentance, and while this may not result in full deliverance from the situation, it will result in the goodness of God's forgiveness.

I'm not proud of this in any way, but since the time the Lord saved my soul, I've had seasons of struggle with sin, namely alcohol consumption. I've suffered unnecessary loss in my life, but can tell you first-hand, that God's goodness is always ready to respond to a repentant heart. There have been times in which I believed God's purpose for my life was ruined, but the fact that I'm writing this right now is evidence that God's purpose is still intact.

Do you sometimes feel as though your future is unclear? That maybe you've "disappointed" God one too many times for Him to still use your life to impact others? Take heart! God knows the plans He has for you, and they are good! Don't stop praying to the Lord. Don't stop fellowshipping with other believers. Don't stop speaking encouraging words to those around you. We serve a good God that only desires we come to Him first instead of searching for our own solutions. God is the source of goodness and does not want us doubting Him nor His great love for us.

Since the beginning of time, the enemy's strategy has been to preoccupy the human race with chasing this world's "good." But as our Lord and Savior Jesus Christ said, there is only One Source of goodness:

> *"And seek not ye what ye shall eat, or what ye shall drink, neither be ye of doubtful mind. For all these things do the nations of the world seek after: and your Father knoweth that ye have need of these things. But rather seek ye the kingdom of God; and all these things shall be added unto you. Fear not, little flock; for it is your Father's good pleasure to give you the kingdom." Luke 12:29-32 KJV*

Printed in the United States
by Baker & Taylor Publisher Services